MUSIC HALLS
TO MOVIE PALACES

by John L. Scherer

An exhibition organized by the New York State Museum, Albany and circulated by
the Gallery Association of New York State

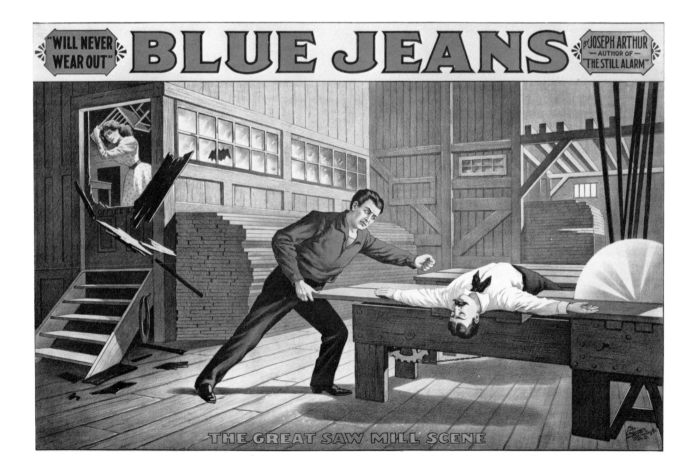

MUSIC HALLS
TO MOVIE PALACES

was organized by the Division of Historical and Anthropological Services from the Theatre Collection of the New York State Museum, State Education Department, Albany, New York.

ABOUT THE
GALLERY ASSOCIATION

The Gallery Association is a non-profit organization that provides traveling exhibitions, art transport, fine arts insurance, and exhibit design services to more than 250 museums and other exhibiting institutions throughout New York State and the surrounding region. For more information, write to the Gallery Association, Box 345, Hamilton, NY 13346, or call (315) 824-2510.

The Gallery Association's programs are made possible by its members, by public funds from the New York State Council on the Arts, New York Council for the Humanities, and National Endowments for the Arts and Humanities, and by contributions from the Agway Foundation, Charles Ulrick and Josephine Bay Foundation, Chemical Bank, The Dow Chemical Company, Gebbie Foundation, General Electric Corporate Research and Development Center, IBM Corporation, Samuel H. Kress Foundation, Metropolitan Life Insurance Co., New York Telephone, Niagara Mohawk Power Corporation, Philip Morris, Inc., The John Ben Snow Memorial Trust, and Tri-Wall.

ISBN 0-934483-07-8

Catalog design: Lenweaver Design
Photography: Courtney Frisse (cover, title page, pp.3, 4, 12, 13, 14, 15, 16, 19, 20, back cover); New York State Museum (pp.7, 8, 10, 22)

MUSIC HALLS
TO MOVIE PALACES

urn-of-the-century Americans entertained themselves by attending the latest production at their local music hall or opera house. The show may have been simply a band concert, or it could have been a new melodrama or musical comedy, fresh from its run in New York City; a well-known actor or actress would have increased the excitement. Another familiar form of opera-house entertainment was the vaudeville show, where audiences could enjoy everything from singing and dancing to comedy skits and juggling acts. Burlesque was yet another feature to behold. Because the local music halls depended on the same small-town audiences, they changed their programs constantly. Most presented a different show almost every night, or at least every weekend. Entertainers were vagabonds who were perennially on the road, providing ever-fresh entertainment to the hinterlands as well as to the major cities.

By 1915, the character of live entertainment had begun to change as the motion picture became increasingly popular. At first movies borrowed their material from melodramas, and became a part of the live entertainment featured in the vaudeville show. Soon the motion picture began to dominate the show, and music halls and vaudeville theatres were supplanted by movie palaces. When the movies learned to talk, live entertainment began to fade, and by 1932, the transition from music hall to movie palace was largely complete.

Before sound came to the movies, live popular entertainment was in its heyday. This survey explores that period by focusing on the wide variety of popular entertainment forms that were available to Americans between 1850 and 1930, drawing on the contents of the Theatre Collection at the New York State Museum.

Before 1850, drama's audience was largely composed of an urban elite; after 1920, movies and radio supplied the public's demand for popular drama, and the theatre returned to its elitist base. So it was that the seventy-year period between 1850 and 1920 was the heyday of popular theatre in America.

During the first half of the nineteenth century, most American theatres tried to offer a wide range of entertainment that would include something for everyone. Soon, however,

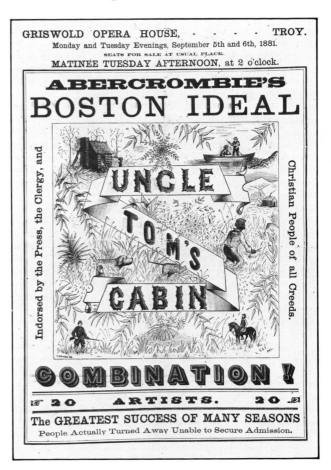

it became clear that there were irreconcilable conflicts in attempting to simultaneously satisfy the tastes of the middle class and the upper class with the same material. The final rift occurred at New York City in 1849. That year, William Macready, a well-known English actor who typified the epitome of the aristocracy and was celebrated by upper-class theatre-goers, was appearing at the Astor Place Opera House. Edwin Forrest, an American actor who portrayed popular heroes and was idolized by the middle class, was also appearing in New York, and working people were urged through broadsides and newspapers to unite and prevent the English theatre from ruling in the city. At Macready's May 10th performance, a melee broke out; thirty-one people were killed and one hundred fifty were injured. After the tragedy, which came to be known as the Astor Place Riot, Macready returned to England, and upper- and middle-class entertainment separated, fragmenting into many pieces.

MELODRAMA

As it evolved, the popular stage reaffirmed the kind of traditional values to which people clung in times of change. The United States was undergoing a transformation from a principally agrarian society to one that was urban and industrial. The plots of popular plays centered on the conflict between virtuous plain people and immoral, conniving businessmen. Melodrama, complete with leering, mustachioed villains and other-worldly heroines, pure of heart but firm of purpose, conveyed a world of fairy tale and fantasy. In its classic form, melodrama forced the heroine to choose between her feelings and her sense of duty—often in the form of posing a choice between her love for a poor but worthy farmboy and her desperate responsibility to redeem the family mortgage by marrying the corrupt villain.

While minor characters provided comic relief, the major characters suffered through a series of predicaments that strained the credibility but delighted the imagination. During the course of a single evening's performance, the hero or heroine could be tied to a railroad track in front of an oncoming locomotive, fed to a buzz saw, trapped in a burning building, or even face a vile threat to her or his honor. There seemed to be no limit to the audience's appetite for such near-disasters. At the end, the plays always arrived at a morally edifying conclusion in which Right, Justice, and Goodness triumphed. Audiences would loudly cheer the scenes they enjoyed and just as loudly deride those that they judged to lack action or interest; in this manner, they helped to shape the play, for the unpopular scenes subsequently would be cut and the popular ones elaborated upon.

In this era before the birth of the motion picture, every town and village contained some arena for live performances. From the large French Renaissance-style music halls and opera houses of the cities and larger towns to the grange halls of the smallest hamlets, melodrama and other forms of live entertainment were performed everywhere. The larger music halls and opera houses contained their auditoriums on the upper floors; shops or banks occupied the street levels. Most music halls possessed a minimum of scenery. The standard equipment would consist of two curtains with side flats: one curtain would have a kitchen scene painted on one side and a forest on the other; the second curtain might feature an elaborate parlor scene and a prison on its reverse. Since the plots of popular melodramas were all so similar, almost any play could be performed with these four scenes as the backdrops.

At the beginning of each performance, the audience was asked to refrain from stamping its feet, eating peanuts, whistling, shouting, standing on chairs, and spitting on the floor. Although genteel observers found them to be unruly, audiences were determined to enjoy themselves, even if they had to entertain one another.

Perhaps the most popular play of the late nineteenth century was *Uncle Tom's Cabin*, which opened in New York City in 1853 and ran for 325 consecutive performances. Based on the novel by Harriet Beecher Stowe, the play describes life on Shelby's idyllic Kentucky plantation, where a slave-trader forces Shelby to sell his slaves in order to pay his debts. When one slave, Eliza Harris, escapes to the North with her young son, an elderly slave known as Uncle Tom refuses to go with them because he feels it is his Christian duty to submit to his superiors. On the way to be sold, Tom meets Little Eva St. Clair, a slaveowner's daughter from a neighboring plantation. She persuades her father to buy Tom. Eva is ill, and troubled deeply by slavery; she dies a slow death, after which Tom is sold at a slave auction to Simon Legree, a particularly brutal slave-driver. After refusing to whip other slaves, Tom dies a martyr's death at Legree's hands. *Uncle Tom's Cabin* enjoyed such popularity that playwrights began taking certain liberties with the plot, and many different versions of the play were produced. New scenes were introduced for the audiences' delight, as were special effects. In one such version, live bloodhounds were introduced on stage to track down Eliza and her son as they escaped.

East Lynne, a dramatization of an English novel, published and adapted for the stage in 1861, proved to be *Uncle Tom's* nearest competition in terms of popularity. Lady Isabel is unjustly accused of infidelity by her own unfaithful husband. Unable to cope with his jealous restrictions, she falls in love and runs away with another man, leaving her husband and her infant son, Willie. To the horror of Victorian audiences, she has shirked her womanly duties, but she gets her just deserts when her lover abandons her. Then, drawn by her maternal instincts, she returns home, in disguise, to visit baby Willie, who, she finds, has contracted a dreadful illness and is on his deathbed. Lady Isabel reveals her true identity and reasserts her deep love for her son; she hears his last breath, gasping "Mama." Then Isabel herself falls ill, and on her own deathbed she is forgiven by her husband.

T. S. Arthur's temperance novel, *Ten Nights In a Barroom*, was the basis of another long-lived melodrama of the same title. The plot concerns the destruction of Joe Morgan and his family by alcohol. After beginning with a few harmless drinks on his way home from work, Joe soon is drawn to spend more and more time at the tavern. One day his daughter, Mary, follows him there and pleads with him to come home, singing this famous refrain:

Father dear Father, come home with me now!
The clock in the steeple strikes one.
You said you were coming right home from the shop

As soon as your day's work was done.
Our fire has gone out, our house's all dark
And Mother's been watching since tea,
With poor brother Benny so sick in her arms,
And none to help her but me.
Come home, come home, come home!
Please Father, dear Father, come home!

As Joe attempts to mooch a drink for the road, someone throws a whiskey glass at him, and it misses and smashes into little Mary's head. A tragic death scene follows, in which Mary again pleads with her father to reform, and he agrees. Joe comforts himself at home with a bottle of whiskey, and then, during an elaborate delirium scene, he remembers his pledge to Mary and dries himself out.

Other popular melodramas detailed the virtues of country life in contrast to the corruptions of the city. *The Old Homestead*, in which Denman Thompson played a character known as Uncle Joshua, was based on such a theme; it was performed between 1876 and 1900. Still others featured romanticized folk heroes and frontiersmen: Joseph Jefferson III appeared in *Rip Van Winkle* between 1865 and 1904, and Frank Mayo played Davy Crockett in the play of the same name from 1872 to 1896. Themes of the American West were always popular.

An honest-to-goodness live frontier hero who began making the music-hall circuit was William F. Cody, better known as Buffalo Bill. His exploits had been made famous during the 1860s in dime novels written by Ned Buntline. In 1872, Buntline convinced Cody to leave Nebraska, where he was fighting in the Indian wars, and star in his new production, *The Scouts of the Plains*. By 1874, Cody had organized his own troupe for *Scouts of the Plains, or Red Deviltry As It Is*. Other plays that followed were *The Knight of the Plains, Buffalo Bill's Last Trail, The Prairie Waif*, and *Buffalo Bill's Last Stand*. All featured Indian war dances, surprise attacks, fierce fighting, heroic rescues, and very little plot. In 1884, Buffalo Bill moved on to bigger and better things, opening his "Wild West Show," which was to receive acclaim throughout the United States and Europe for over a quarter century.

BROADWAY

Most of the plays that toured the country originated in New York City, the nation's entertainment capital, where they played before acting companies took them on the road, or before they were eventually performed by local companies. Perhaps it was the producer Charles Frohman who, more than any other individual, was responsible for the American popular theatre as it was at the turn of the century. Between 1890 and 1915, Frohman produced more than five hundred plays in New York, London, and Paris. He initiated a new type of star system and collaborated with most of the leading playwrights of the era. It was a happy time for Broadway, and for the colorful theatre personalities who were so much a part of it.

Frohman came to New York from Sandusky, Ohio in 1877 when he joined his brother, Daniel, in managing the Madison Square Theatre. Later he organized the Charles Frohman Stock Company, and by 1890 he had become a fixture on the Broadway scene. Frohman opened the Empire Theatre on Broadway at 40th Street in 1893, one of the first theatres to move uptown on Broadway; it was to become the street's first "star factory." Until then, most of the major theatrical stars were of middle age, for it had taken them years to achieve their high status. Frohman believed that the public was ready to worship younger performers: "Romance instead of respect" was the way he phrased it. His most famous protege was a nonchalant young man named John Drew.

Drew was the public's idea of a gentleman, the man of eternal good manners,

CHARLES FROHMAN PRESENTS

JOHN DREW
IN W. SOMERSET MAUGHAM'S COMEDY
Jack Straw

"Don't stand there grinning like a Cheshire cat!"

faultless breeding, and unvarying grace. At a time when acting was not considered a respectable career, Drew bridged the gap between the world of the theatre and high society, engaging in such aristocratic pursuits as polo and tennis, sports hitherto reserved almost exclusively for the rich.

Another Frohman star of the first magnitude was Maude Adams, an actress whom Frohman succeeded in bending to his every wish, dictating even her private life. Adams had spent her entire life in the theatre, appearing first at the age of nine months in *The Lost Child*. Frohman engaged her in William Gillette's *All the Comforts of Home*, and after playing opposite John Drew in other Frohman productions, she became a major star with her appearance in James Matthew Barrie's *The Little Minister* in 1897. Her most famous role was as Peter Pan in Barrie's play of the same name, a character she played more than 1,500 times following its opening at the Empire Theatre in 1905. Maude Adams, John Drew, and other leading stars were among those who brought

Broadway to every section of the nation with traveling troupes. Thus the stars received the same widespread exposure as the plays, and their names became household words.

David Belasco, Charles Frohman's nearest rival as a producer, was also a playwright and an actor. Saturated with the stage and all things dramatic, he had decided that the best contrast to his flamboyant personality was the white-collared garb of the Roman Catholic priest. Affecting similar clothing, he became known as the "Bishop of Broadway."

In 1896, Belasco wrote—as well as produced—one of his most successful plays, *The Heart of Maryland*, starring his celebrated protege, Mrs. Leslie Carter. After divorcing the millionaire Carter of Carter's Little Liver Pills, the flame-haired belle had turned to Belasco to launch her career as an actress. *The Heart of Maryland* cast Mrs. Carter as the heroine, Maryland Calvert, opposite a hero played by Maurice Barrymore—the father of Lionel, Ethel, and John. The play's climax came when Mrs. Carter silenced a bell in a forty-foot bell

tower by clinging precariously to its clapper, an action that allowed Barrymore, in the role of a Union soldier unjustly accused of spying, to escape. The use of the bell tower illustrates Belasco's love of realism for the stage. In his play, *The Woman*, he reproduced the lobby of a Washington hotel, complete with a switchboard and phone booths. Offstage, an elevator could be heard operating, while through a window on the set, the audience viewed a picture of the Capitol dome.

The leading American playwright of the time was Clyde Fitch, a prolific author who, at the peak of his career, wrote enough to keep several managers busy. The night his *The Truth* opened, on January 7, 1907, four other Fitch plays were running simultaneously in New York, establishing a record no other playwright has ever achieved. Fitch's *Nathan Hale*, *Major Andre*, and *Barbara Frietchie* took full advantage of the rage for historical and costume romances. *Barbara Frietchie*, the first Fitch/Frohman collaboration, was the greatest success on Broadway in 1900. Like David Belasco, Clyde Fitch had an affection for realism in stage sets. *Captain Jinks of the Horse Marines*, Ethel Barrymore's first success, boasted a replica of the lobby of New York's Hotel Brevoort as it had been in 1870.

Another important playwright of the era was William Gillette, also an actor and director, who, with the exception of John Drew, was Frohman's most formidable male star. Frohman booked the road company of Gillette's first great success, *Held by the Enemy*, and then personally produced its comedy successor, *Too Much Johnson*. The austere and unapproachable Gillette, famous for his portrayal of Sherlock Holmes, rivaled Drew as the first gentleman of the American theatre.

Like William F. Cody, many performers of the time had already achieved fame before they embarked on an acting career. Two such "actors" were the prizefighters Gentleman Jim Corbett and John L. Sullivan, both of whom appeared in plays directed by their fight managers.

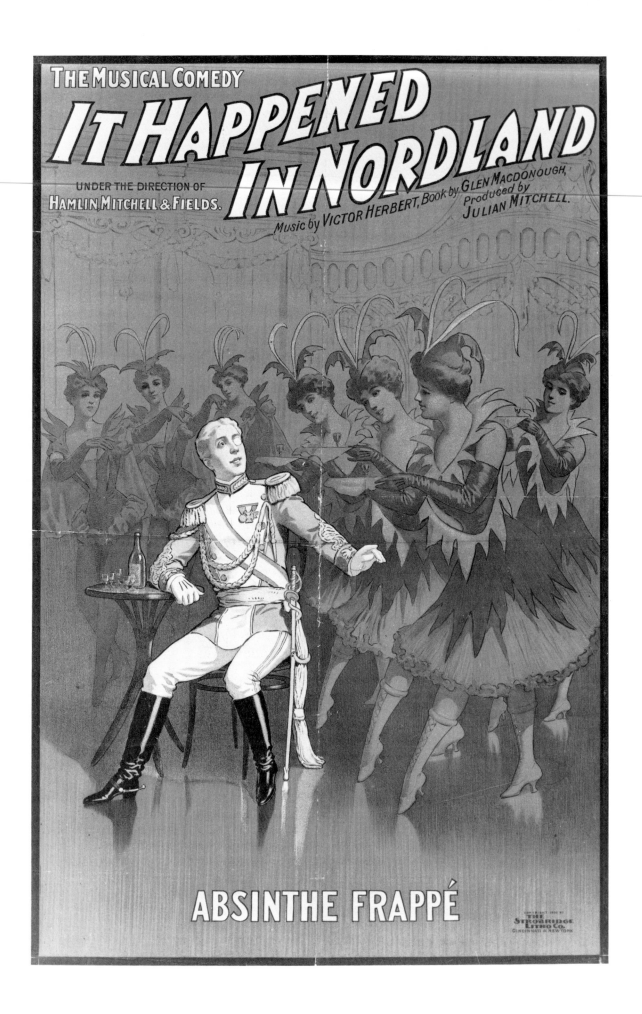

MUSICAL COMEDIES

I n 1866, Henry C. Jarrett, a New York City theatre manager, and Harry Palmer, a Wall Street broker, brought a European ballet troupe to America and outfitted it with beautiful sets and sensual costumes. Unfortunately, the Academy of Music, in which the performance was to be held, caught fire and burned, and the only other suitable theatre in New York was Niblo's Garden, where a melodrama entitled *The Black Crook* was being performed. William Wheatly, the stage manager at Niblo's, was unsure about his shaky new production and proposed the idea of combining the two shows. The resulting combination of European ballet and spectacle with a melodrama loosely based on *Faust* is acknowledged as the first major step toward burlesque and musical comedy. As it developed during the late nineteenth century, musical comedy covered a wide range. There was the spectacular that consisted of a lavish production set in an exotic land, such as *Around the World in Eighty Days*; the play that centered on the daily lives of ordinary Americans, which included catchy songs, dances, and exciting new heroes; and the European-based operetta, which transported Americans into the upper-class world of elegance, grace, and order.

Perhaps the most popular musical comedy in the category that presented daily life was Hoyt's *A Trip to Chinatown*. The play opened in New York in 1890 and ran for 650 performances, the longest run of any nineteenth-century production in the nation's entertainment capital. Traveling companies carried it throughout the nation. Set in San Francisco's Chinatown, it follows the adventures of a young man and his uncle as each plans a rendezvous with the same young woman at the same restaurant. They end up in different dining rooms, but the waiter confuses the orders and the young couple end up hiding from the uncle. The reason for the play's success was the music; as in previous Hoyt comedies, it had almost nothing to do with the plot and was, in fact, billed as "musical interruptions." The songs made popular by *A Trip to Chinatown* include "The Bowery! The Bowery," and "Reuben, Reuben, I've Been Thinking." The composer Charles K. Harris paid Hoyt five hundred dollars and a share of the royalties to incorporate his shaky new song, "After the Ball," into the play. Although, like most of the other music, it bore little relation to the narrative, it was an instant success, and became the first popular song to sell five million copies of sheet music.

The Prince of Pilsen was an example of the third type of musical, the European-based operetta. The plot concerns a midwestern beer brewer who vacations in Spain and is mistaken for a student prince who is vacationing in the same area. The king of this kind of musical was Victor Herbert, who composed hundreds of songs and wrote the scores of several successful light operas. His songs, with their sentimental lyrics and their lilting melodies, made him the most popular composer of his time. In 1900, he wrote the music for *The Singing Girl*; in 1903, *Babes in Toyland*; in 1904, *It Happened in Nordland*. In 1905, Herbert had a rousing hit entitled *Mlle. Modiste*, starring Fritzi Scheff, whose backless gowns and torrid singing of "Kiss Me Again" set male hearts aflutter. Inspired by the success of Franz Lehar's *The Merry Widow*, Herbert wrote *The Red Mill* in 1907, a light opera that is still periodically revived and enjoyed by musical audiences.

BURLESQUE

Burlesque was born in New York City when women, wearing tights, posed as living statuary in 1847-1848. The exploitation of female sexuality in American show business developed gradually. Displays of women's bodies were first featured only in disreputable variety houses, but they soon received additional public exposure in elaborate musicals and in traveling troupes of women doing parodies—"burlesques"—while wearing revealing clothing. Eventually, the American burlesque show evolved: a girlie show with female sexuality as a major theme. Burlesque's competition with other entertainment forms compelled it to become more and more risque until it culminated with the striptease.

Agnes Evans and Nettie Huffman, who worked as a team, were two of the most popular burlesque stars of the 1880s and 1890s. Evans wore magnificent costumes, some of them rather risque by nineteenth-century standards, many of which she designed herself. Her partner, Nettie Huffman, was a male impersonator who dressed the part of a handsome young man. It was not unusual for females to play male roles in the theatre at the time, so this was an accepted form of entertainment. Female impersonators were also popular. Evans and Huffman were considered the best-dressed ladies in burlesque, and one of the finest of the singing specialty teams. A review of their "Don Jose" that concluded the burlesque at the Lyceum Theatre in New York about 1890 indicated that the hit of the show was the act by "Agnes Evans and Nettie Huffman, travesty burlesque stars, whose talents, as well as handsome wardrobes, were the mag-

nets which have won them renown." Miss Huffman portrayed a Castilian lover named Don Jose, and Miss Evans the flirty Donna Gregara. A review of another skit also applauded their performance: "Agnes Evans and Nettie Huffman, who lead Sam T. Jack's Extravaganza Company, which will be seen at the Globe Opera House tonight, might justly claim the title of 'Queens of Burlesque.' Two prettier women, or better dressed, or more clever in voice and action, never graced a comic stage."

Agnes Evans.   503

Newsboy   NEW YORK.

The first burlesque star actually to be crowned a "Queen" was May Howard. After starring in several shows, in 1888 she formed her own company, which she called "a leg show pure and simple." The stocky woman with large thighs was the ideal until the turn of the century, and Howard would employ no woman who weighed less than 150 pounds. Some female performers were even accused of using padding. Later, the broad-hipped, big-busted woman would lose favor to the thin, long-legged chorus-girl image. Little Egypt's cootch dance at the Chicago World's Fair in 1893 added the belly dance as a distinctive feature of burlesque.

Burlesque was a combination of song, dance, humor, and comedy skits. In order to compete with the popularity of vaudeville and the revue, into both of which its forms eventu-

ally would be incorporated, burlesque by the early 1900s had to revitalize its "dirty jokes" and broad sexual skits. The result was the striptease, a combination of naked skin, suggestion, and seduction. Until the striptease was born, burlesque performers generally continued to wear tights: Truly Shattuck advertised in the 1890s that she had introduced a specialty in which she would change on stage from full costume to tights.

14

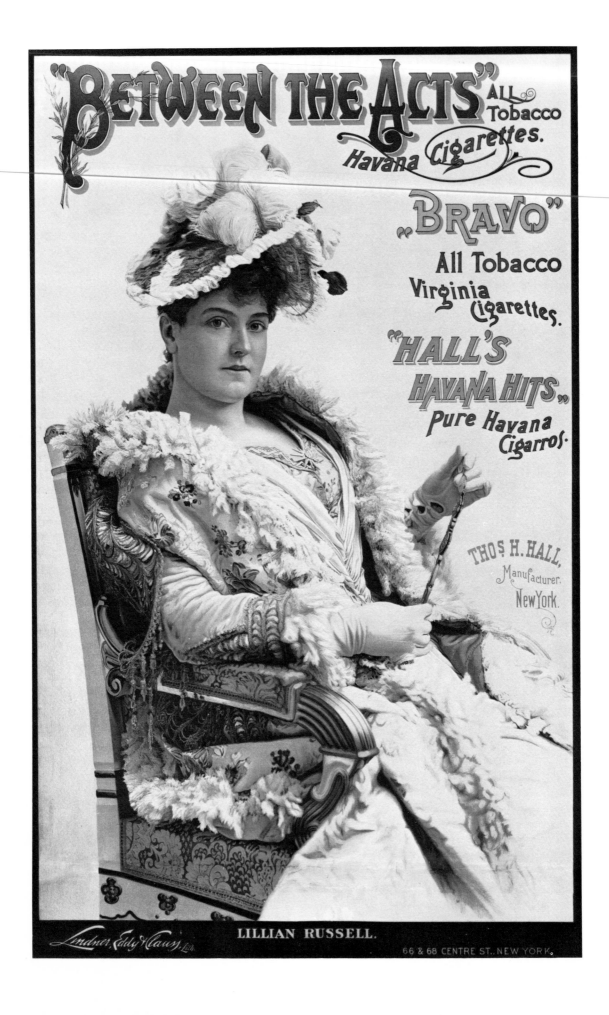

VAUDEVILLE

The term "vaudeville" is French and refers to a light pastoral play with musical interludes. The American vaudeville show had its beginning when saloon owners sponsored free variety shows to attract customers. The early versions had a bad reputation, for they included girlie shows; promoters expanded these variety shows, moved them into theatres, cleaned up their reputation by deleting objectionable material, and began advertising them as family entertainment. By the 1890s, the new form of variety show, now called "vaudeville," was the most popular entertainment form in the United States. Favorite acts featured singing, dancing, animal performances, magic, and humor—especially ethnic humor.

The man who gave vaudeville its biggest boost came from a background of minstrel shows and the circus. Tony Pastor, considered the father of American vaudeville, moved his theatre from New York's Bowery area to Broadway in 1875, and then to his 14th Street Theatre in 1881. Here his variety shows were billed as "high class," and Pastor tried to establish a family audience. He encouraged women to attend his performances by offering expensive door-prizes like sewing machines, hats, and dresses. He also offered more modest gifts, such as dress patterns or sewing kits, for every female patron. Pastor's most famous star was the charming Lillian Russell. Other theatre managers soon began to follow his lead.

The two men who made vaudeville a big business on a national scale also came from a circus background. Benjamin Keith and Edward Albee built their entertainment empire on three basic components: by eliminating offensive material, they aimed their shows at the family audience; they initiated the continuous show, beginning performances at 9:30 a.m. and continuing until 10:30 p.m. (the shows would open with "chasers," the most uninteresting performances on the program, to help move people in and out of the theatre); and they associated the genre with luxury, building such palatial showplaces as the Colonial Theatre in Boston in 1894, where, for 25¢, you were a king. Keith and Albee joined with other theatre owners to form the United Booking Office, which booked all performers exclusively for their member theatres, a practice that was similar to other theatre monopolies.

Vaudeville became extremely popular, and vaudeville theatres, separately and in chains, sprang up everywhere. In 1896 there were seven vaudeville theatres in New York City; by 1910, there were thirty-one. In 1913, the Palace opened at 47th and Broadway, and it was to remain the most prestigious vaudeville theatre in the nation. Frederick F. Proctor (1851-1929) owned some fifty theatres, mostly in the New York area, but also in upstate New York cities as well as in Boston, Hartford, and Montreal. He had begun his career as an acrobat and aerialist under the stage name of Frederick F. Levantine. Proctor started his entrepreneurial career managing theatres after he returned to his home in Nassau, New York from a second European tour as "Equilibrist of the 70's" in 1880. During the 1880s, he leased or acquired several Albany, New York theatres. In 1896, he opened Proctor's Pleasure Palace on 23rd Street in New York, the first theatre devoted exclusively to vaudeville. For a short time, he joined forces with his rival, B.F. Keith, and formed the Keith and Proctor Amusement Co., which broke up in 1911. When a Proctor's Theatre in Albany opened on April 6, 1917, an advertising flyer announced that "This house of variety will stand as a monument to moral entertainment of the Proctor sort." Proctor sold his chain to Radio-Keith Orpheum Corp. in 1929 for 16 million dollars. He is acknowledged as the dean of vaudeville theatre managers.

Because theatres across the country constantly needed fresh faces and new talent, performers were constantly on the road. The salaries of vaudeville stars exploded: Eva Tanguay, who was born in Cohoes, New York in 1878 and made her debut at the Cohoes Music Hall in 1882, was a major vaudeville star by 1900, earning $3,500 per week. She exuded an aura of untamed female sexuality and was referred to as "The Queen of Perpetual Motion." Tanguay was an image of total abandon when she sang her famous signature number, "I Don't Care." Other major stars who traveled to every corner of the United States were Lillian Russell, Elsie Janis, Nora Bayes, Marilyn Miller, Sophie Tucker, Mae West, Fanny Brice, Bert Lahr, Al Jolson, Eddie Cantor, the comedian team of Joe Weber and Lew Fields, who strongly influenced vaudeville's developing ethnic comedy, and Joe Cook, who was billed as the "One-Man Vaudeville Show."

Cook was one of America's most beloved comedians during the first half of the twentieth century. His career peaked when he starred in musical comedy on Broadway in *Rain or Shine* in 1928 and in *Fine and Dandy* in 1930. This versatile performer's climb to the top encompassed just about every type of show that regaled audiences during the heyday of live popular entertainment in America. Not only did he star in musical comedy, but he headlined in vaudeville and also appeared in burlesque and in films.

Cook began his career in vaudeville in 1906 by responding to a newspaper advertisement placed by a New York City theatre manager who was searching for fresh talent. To get an audition, he faked a photograph of himself juggling seventeen balls. The theatre manager was so impressed with his juggling, globe-rolling, and tightrope-walking that he did not even care when he found out that the applicant could juggle only eight balls. He was hired to perform in the Keith Theatres, and while touring on this circuit, Cook picked up more stunts and learned to play a variety of musical instruments. After he injured his ankle, he was unable to dance, walk a wire, or perform any of his famous balancing and juggling stunts, but

turning adversity into opportunity, he hauled out some burned cork and developed a blackface comedy act, brimming with nonsensical chatter. When the audience applauded heartily, the spontaneous stream of patter became a hallmark of his act.

When his ankle healed, Cook put aside his cork and devised one of the longest single acts ever presented on a vaudeville stage: "Joe Cook's One-Man Vaudeville Show." With boundless enthusiasm, he juggled, walked the wire, painted, and played musical instruments to the accompaniment of a staccato line of chatter. The act also featured such crazy contraptions as a guitar rigged to spring apart when he played it, presaging Jimmy Durante's collapsing piano. With the audience warmed up by his non-stop zest, Cook proceeded to tell his famous comic stories. Audiences howled at the tall tale of Delehanty, who hit a home run that traveled five miles, enabling him to tally 362 runs before the fielders could return the ball.

In 1919, Cook went from vaudeville to musical comedy, where he appeared with Raymond Hitchcock in *Kitchy Koo*. His big break in musicals came when Earl Carroll signed him on as star of the first edition of the *Vanities* in 1923, a musical revue that became a thirteen-year tradition in New York City. Cook played in three of its editions, starring with such noted performers as Peggy Hopkins Joyce and Sophie Tucker. Like many vaudeville stars, Joe Cook went into radio and motion pictures during the 1930s. He retired from show business in 1942.

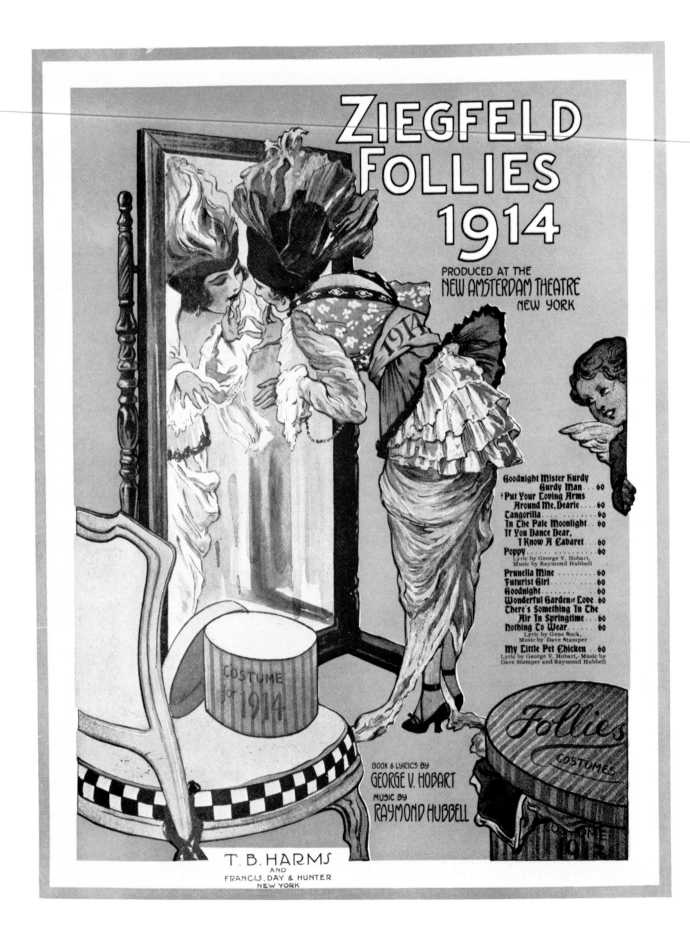

ZIEGFELD

I n 1907, Florenz Ziegfeld combined elements of vaudeville, burlesque, and musical comedy into a revue that glorified the American woman; he called it *The Ziegfeld Follies*. The idea was the inspiration of Anna Held, a Parisian music-hall singer, whom Ziegfeld had met on a trip to Europe in 1895. Ziegfeld brought Held to America, and shortly after her arrival, they married. It was the beginning of a successful fourteen-year partnership.

Ziegfeld introduced Held to the American public in the play *A Parlor Match*. It was an instant hit, and soon, under his direction Held became the best-known theatre personality in New York. Her tiny waistline, her mischievous eyes, and her extravagant style of living soon had the whole town talking. She took baths in milk and spent huge amounts of money on clothes. In 1898 when she played the lead in *Papa's Wife*, her costumes alone were said to have cost over $40,000. When she sang "Won't You Come and Play Wiz Me?" and "I Just Can't Make My Eyes Behave," Anna Held epitomized for Americans all the Gallic spice and naughtiness of the French stage.

The Ziegfeld Follies introduced many other stars to the stage, and Ziegfeld was responsible for launching many of the era's most popular songs with his lavish production numbers. Eddie Cantor, Helen Morgan, Fanny Brice, W.C. Fields, Ed Wynn, Marilyn Miller, Nora Bayes, and a host of others began their careers in the *Follies*, which continued to run at the New Amsterdam Theatre in New York until Ziegfeld's death in 1932. While the *Follies* appealed to the masses, a more sophisticated type of entertainment entitled *The Midnight Frolics* was offered on the rooftop of the New Amsterdam. Ziegfeld began the *Frolics* in 1915 to cater to a wealthier clientele; Will Rogers got his start here, as did a young couple who billed themselves as "The Glorias."

Adelaide and Albert Gloria, brother and sister, had just come from Germany in 1915 where they had been billed as the fastest dance team in the world. Their first American appearance was in a lavish production with John Philip Sousa at New York's Hippodrome. Discovered by Ziegfeld, the Glorias were soon employed for *The Midnight Frolics*. (Like other entertainers, they collected photographs and autographs from fellow performers, accumulating a rather extensive collection of theatre memorabilia, much of which is now in the New York State Museum Theatre Collection.) When the *Frolics* succumbed to Prohibition, the Glorias continued their career on the vaudeville circuit, also appearing occasionally in musical comedy.

The Ziegfeld Follies continued to be popular until the Depression, and was imitated in theatres throughout the nation. Women everywhere craved the glamour of being a "Ziegfeld Girl." Florenz Ziegfeld's accomplishment was to create a spectacle of beauty combined with a show that offered something for everybody.

Leontine in Trouble.

PATHÉ

THE SHIELDING SHADOW
THE WONDER SERIAL
BY GEO. B. SEITZ
THROUGH BOLTED DOORS
5TH EPISODE
FEATURING
GRACE DARMOND
RALPH KELLARD AND LEON BARY
PRODUCED BY ASTRA FILM CORP.

MOVIES

Thomas Edison first projected a moving picture on his Vita-scope in 1896. By 1910, most cities had opened one or more small movie houses, called "nick-elodeons". Motion pictures were so popular that enor-mous theatres had to be constructed to ac-commodate the crowds. These new movie palaces were an elaboration of earlier vaudeville houses, and actually were built to accommodate live acts as well as movies. The continuous performance merely added movies to its bill of fare, offering a combination of both.

Inside these palatial new theatres, audi-ences found refuge from the ugliness of the cit-ies and from the boredom of life. Movies were silent until 1927, and for the most part their plots were identical to those of the melodra-mas that were performed on the stage. The films were accompanied by appropriate music, played on either a piano or, in the larger thea-tres, on a huge pipe organ that would make the very walls vibrate. Some of the early films even had special music composed to be played while they were being shown. Until the late 1920s, it was not Hollywood but New York and its environs that were the center of the film industry. Movies were made in sound stages in New York City, Long Island, and New Jersey.

Two styles of movie palace architecture evolved. The standard school had its prece-dent in the opera house and vaudeville theatre, but it grew more exotic as it advanced. Its most avid proponent was the architect Thomas Lamb, whose classical designs became a sym-bol of the era. He was best known for his abil-ity to create a world of illusion in a movie thea-tre and is considered the dean of the standard school. Lamb's early theatres were simple and delicate in design, but after 1929 he employed the Italian Baroque style. He designed more than three hundred theatres which were con-structed in all parts of the world. Among those he designed in New York State were the Re-gent (1913), the Strand (1914), the Rivoli (1917), all in Albany; Loew's State (1929) in Syracuse; and Proctor's (1926) in Schenectady.

The atmospheric school of movie palace architecture borrowed from nature and from the more flamboyant landscape gardeners of the past. The architect John Eberson was the chief proponent of this style and is considered its dean. He created amphitheatres that were roofed by moonlit skies in which stars were visible and clouds drifted by. The theme might be an Italian garden, a Persian court, a Spanish patio, or a mystical Egyptian temple yard. Eberson was the architect of more than five hundred theatres throughout the world. One, the Palace in Albany, New York, opened in 1931. Fashioned in Eberson's Austrian Baroque style, it contains a balcony that extends over two-thirds of the auditorium. The Depression eventually phased out the construction of movie palaces, but many of them, including Albany's Palace, survive today and attract new audiences to appreciate them.

When Proctor's opened in Schenectady on December 27, 1926, the feature film was *Stranded in Paris*, starring Bebe Daniels and James Hall. The vaudeville bill included "A Family Revue" with Mr. and Mrs. Norman Phil-ips, who had just completed an engagement with *George White's Scandals*; The Sunshine Boys, "a triple alliance of song, music and fun;" Joe Weston and Harriet Hutchins doing char-acter impersonations; and Carl Shaw and Jean

Carroll in "Dance Manners." All this entertainment was available for an admission price of 35¢ for the matinee and 50¢ for the evening performance.

Until the late 1920s, movies and radio had not seriously challenged live entertainment. Movies brought the sight of great stars, and radio carried their sounds to every corner of the nation, but only live productions contained both elements. In 1927, sound came to the movies with *The Jazz Singer*; it was there that Al Jolson delivered his famous line, "You ain't heard nuthin yet." With the advent of the "talkies," the course of live popular entertainment began to change. Its death was portended in 1932, when movies finally claimed the Palace Theatre in New York. Although vaudeville performances continued, in combination with the movies, until the 1940s, the live portion of the show was in a steady decline. As the movies improved with modern technology and a new breed of stars and directors, the competition became too tough, and vaudeville, melodrama, and other forms of live entertainment succumbed. Television dealt it the final death blow.

Reminders of this lively era of popular entertainment survive today in the form of colorful posters and broadsides that were plastered to buildings and fences or circulated among the crowds to advertise and promote the shows. Many of the most interesting posters were lithographed by Strobridge Litho Company of Cincinnati and New York between 1890 and 1918. Programs also survive in abundance, as do the memorabilia of the performers themselves. These artifacts convey the vitality and the naivete of the era that produced them, an era that will forever be identified with the kind of live entertainment that appealed to everyone.

BIBLIOGRAPHY

Appelbaum, Stanley. *Scenes From the 19th Century Stage In Advertising Woodcuts.* New York: Dover Publications, Inc., 1977.

Blum, Daniel C. *A Pictorial History of the American Theatre, 1860-1970.* New York: Crown Publishers, 1969.

Carter, Randolph. *The World of Flo Ziegfeld.* New York: Praeger Publishers, 1974.

Churchhill, Allen. *The Great White Way: A Recreation of Broadway's Golden Era of Theatrical Entertainment.* New York: Dutton, 1962.

Farnsworth, Marjorie. *The Ziegfeld Follies.* New York: Bonanza Books, 1956.

Gilbert, Douglas. *American Vaudeville: Its Life and Times.* New York: McGraw-Hill, 1940.

Grimsted, David. *Melodrama Unveiled: American Theatre and Culture, 1800-1850.* Chicago: University of Chicago Press, 1968.

Hall, Ben M. *The Best Remaining Seats: The Story of the Golden Age of the Movie Palace.* New York: Bramhall House, 1961.

Hewitt, Barnard Wolcott. *Theatre U.S.A., 1668 to 1957.* New York: McGraw-Hill, 1959.

Hoyt, Harlowe R. *Town Hall Tonight: Intimate Memories of the Grassroots Days of the American Theatre.* New York: Bramhall House, 1961.

Matlaw, Myron, ed. *American Popular Entertainment: Papers and Proceedings of the Conference on the History of American Popular Entertainment.* Westport, Conn.: Greenwood Press, 1977.

Moody, Richard. *The Astor Place Riot.* Bloomington: Indiana University Press, 1958.

Pearce, Sam. *Stars of the New York Stage, 1870-1970.* A special exhibition sponsored by the Friends of the Theatre and Music Collection, Museum of the City of New York. New York: Museum of the City of New York, 1970.

Scherer, John L. "Broadway's Happiest Time." *Naho* 6:4 (Winter 1973-74), pp.12-15. Albany: New York State Museum.

———. "Funnyman." *Naho* 13:1 and 13:2 (Spring- Summer 1981), pp.53-55. Albany: New York State Museum.

Sobel, Bernard. *Burleycue: An Underground History of Burlesque Days.* New York: Farrar & Rinehart, Inc., 1931.

———. *A Pictorial History of Vaudeville.* New York: The Citadel Press, 1961.

Toll, Robert C. *On With The Show: The First Century of Show Business In America.* New York: Oxford University Press, 1976.

Ward, Morehouse. *Matinee Tomorrow: Fifty Years of Our Theatre.* New York: Whittlesey House, 1949.

CHECKLIST

Melodrama

*Poster for *Only A Shop Girl*, 1902, Strobridge Litho Co., Cincinnati and New York. 38″ x 28″. (Cover illustration)

*Poster for *Blue Jeans*, c. 1890. 28″ x 42 ¼″. (Title page illustration)

*Broadside for a new version of *Uncle Tom's Cabin* as performed at the Griswold Opera House, Troy, N.Y., September 5 and 6, 1881. 14″ x 10 ⅜″. (Illustrated p.3)

*Poster for *East Lynne*, c. 1900, National Pr. & Eng. Co., Chicago, Ill. 27 ¾″ x 21 ¼″. (Illustrated p.4)

Poster for *Gambler of the West*, 1906, Strobridge Litho Co., Cincinnati and New York. 28 ½″ x 19″.

Poster for *The War of Wealth*, 1896, Strobridge Litho Co., Cincinnati and New York. 81″ x 38 ½″.

Poster for *Way Down East*, 1901, Strobridge Litho Co., Cincinnati and New York. 39″ x 29″.

Poster for *Only A Shop Girl*, 1902, Strobridge Litho Co., Cincinnati and New York. 28 ¾″ x 38 ¾″.

Poster for *M'Liss*, 1900, Strobridge Litho Co., Cincinnati and New York. 28 ¾″ x 38 ¾″.

Program for *M'Liss*, Standard Theatre, 1880. 14 ¾″ x 10 ½″.

Poster for *As Ye Sow*, 1906, Strobridge Litho Co., Cincinnati and New York. 38 ½″ x 28 ¾″.

Poster for *Ben Hur*, 1912, Strobridge Litho Co., Cincinnati and New York. 29″ x 19 ½″.

Window card for *Ben Hur*, 1901, Strobridge Litho Co., Cincinnati and New York. 9″ x 14″.

Poster for *Parted On Her Bridal Tour*, 1907, Strobridge Litho Co., Cincinnati and New York. 28 ¾″ x 38 ¾″.

Poster for *Darkest Russia*, 1894, Strobridge Litho Co., Cincinnati and New York. 29″ x 19″.

Poster for *The Waif's Paradise*, 1904, Strobridge Litho Co., Cincinnati and New York. 28 ¾″ x 38 ¾″.

Poster for *Child Slaves of New York*, 1903, Strobridge Litho Co., Cincinnati and New York. 28 ½″ x 38 ½″.

Broadway

Programs for three Broadway theatres, the Savoy (1906), the Belasco (1907), and the Gaiety (1908). Each 9″ x 6″.

Poster for *The Hand of Destiny*, 1896, Strobridge Litho Co., Cincinnati and New York. 28 ¾″ x 19 ¼″.

Program for a performance at Charles Frohman's Empire Theatre, 1918. 9″ x 6″.

*Poster for John Drew in *Jack Straw*, 1908, Strobridge Litho Co., Cincinnati and New York. 81″ x 38″. (Illustrated p.7)

Poster featuring Maude Adams, 1912, Strobridge Litho Co., Cincinnati and New York. 81 ½″ x 31 ½″.

Photographs of Maude Adams as Peter Pan, c. 1905. 5 ½″ x 3″, 5 ¼″ x 3 ¼″, and 5 ½″ x 3 ¼″.

Poster for Nazimova in *Bella Donna*, 1912, Strobridge Litho Co., Cincinnati and New York. 81 ½″ x 39″.

Poster for Billie Burke in *The Runaway*, 1911, Strobridge Litho Co., Cincinnati and New York. 33″ x 25″.

Window card for May Irwin, 1916, Strobridge Litho Co., Cincinnati and New York. 21″ x 13 ½″.

Window card for Ruth Chatterton in *Daddy Long-Legs*, 1914, Strobridge Litho Co., Cincinnati and New York. 22″ x 14″.

Window card for Henrietta Crosman as Mistress Nell, 1900, Strobridge Litho Co., Cincinnati and New York. 28″ x 18″.

Autographed photographs of May Irwin and Henrietta Crosman, c. 1903. Each 6 ½″ x 4 ¼″.

Poster for *The Woman*, 1911, Strobridge Litho Co., Cincinnati and New York. 39″ x 28 ½″.

*Poster for *The Heart of Maryland*, 1904, Strobridge Litho Co., Cincinnati and New York. 19 ½″ x 29.″ (Illustrated p.8)

Silver pill box, souvenir of the 200th performance of *The Heart of Maryland*, at the Herald Square Theatre, c. 1904. 1 ½″ x 2″.

Poster for *Captain Jinks of the Horse Marines*, 1902, Strobridge Litho Co., Cincinnati and New York. 81 ¾″ x 39″.

Poster for *Barbara Frietchie*, 1900, Strobridge Litho Co., Cincinnati and New York. 28 ¾″ x 38 ½″.

Poster for *Secret Service*, 1896, Strobridge Litho Co., Cincinnati and New York. 28 ½" x 19 ¼".

Poster for *Held By The Enemy*, c. 1900, Strobridge Litho Co., Cincinnati and New York. 28 ½" x 38 ½".

Poster for *A Naval Cadet*, 1895, Strobridge Litho Co., Cincinnati and New York. 29" x 19 ½".

On Broadway After The Theatre, from *Harper's Weekly*, December 26, 1891. 16" x 11 ⅛".

After the Theatre, Stopping at the Waldorf-Astoria for Supper, from *Harper's Weekly*, c. 1900. 15 ¾" x 21 ¾".

Musical Comedies

Program for *The Black Crook*, 1866. 15" x 11".

Lithograph of ballet scene from *The Black Crook*, c. 1875. 12" x 9".

Program for *Around the World in 80 Days* at Niblo's Garden Theatre, New York, c. 1880. 14" x 10 ½".

Poster for *The Alaskan*, 1907, Strobridge Litho Co., Cincinnati and New York. 30" x 20".

*Poster for *A Trip to Chinatown*, c. 1890, Strobridge Litho Co., Cincinnati and New York. 38 ½" x 28 ½". (Illustrated p.12)

Poster for *A Milk White Flag*, c. 1900, Strobridge Litho Co., Cincinnati and New York. 30" x 40".

Poster for *The Golden Girl*, c. 1915, Morgan Litho Co., Cleveland, Ohio. 35 ½" x 25 ½".

Poster for *The Prince of Pilsen*, 1902, Strobridge Litho Co., Cincinnati and New York. 29" x 38 ¾".

*Poster for *It Happened In Nordland*, 1905, Strobridge Litho Co., Cincinnati and New York. 28 ½" x 19 ½". (Illustrated p.10)

Poster for *Erminie*, c. 1890, Strobridge Litho Co., Cincinnati and New York. 38 ¾" x 28 ¾".

Poster for *Miss Hook of Holland*, 1908, Strobridge Litho Co., Cincinnati and New York. 38 ½" x 28 ½".

Burlesque

*Pages from a scrapbook kept by burlesque queen Agnes Evans, c. 1895. 10 ¾" x 13 ½". (Illustrated p.14-15)

Poster featuring male impersonator Nettie Huffman in *The Night Owls Beauty Show*, c. 1890. 28" x 14 ¼".

*Photographs of burlesque queen Agnes Evans, c. 1890. 6 ½" x 4 ¼" and 6" x 4 ¼". (Illustrated p.13)

Costume sketches from Agnes Evans' sketchbooks, c. 1897. 5 ⅝" x 8 ⅞", two 8 ¾" x 5 ½", and 5" x 8".

Program for The Empire Theatre, a popular burlesque theatre in Albany, N.Y., c. 1915. 9 ⅛" x 6 ⅛".

Ink blotters advertising The Empire Theatre, Albany, N.Y., c. 1915. 9 ½" x 4" and 4" x 9 ⅛".

Vaudeville

Poster featuring the Orphean Family vocalists at the American Museum, New York, 1844. 17 ¾" x 12".

*Poster featuring a full vaudeville bill at Harry Miner's American Variety Theatre, New York, for Monday, April 8, 1878. 27 ¼" x 10 ½". (Illustrated, back cover)

Poster featuring vaudeville performers at The Rink, Utica, N.Y., for September 1877. 42" x 14".

Poster featuring a vaudeville performance at the Grand Central Theatre, Troy, N.Y., for January 26, 1880. 42" x 14".

*Photograph of the Kaufmann Troupe, c. 1890. 5 ½" x 8 ¾". (Illustrated p.19)

Photograph of performer playing musical glasses, c. 1890. 6 ½" x 4 ¼".

Photograph of a vaudeville act, c. 1890. 9" x 11".

*Tobacco poster picturing vaudeville star Lillian Russell, c. 1890. 25" x 15 ¼". (Illustrated p.16)

Photograph of B.F. Keith's Theatre, c. 1910. 9" x 7".

Program for B.F. Keith's Palace Theatre, New York, featuring Bessie McCoy Davis, for Monday, October 7, 1918. 10" x 4 ¾".

Dance shoes that belonged to vaudeville entertainer Joe Cook.

Photograph of Joe Cook performing his juggling act, c. 1910. 7 ¾" x 6".

Photograph of Joe Cook pointing to a broadside featuring his performance, c. 1914. 7" x 5".

Photograph of a comical Rube Goldberg-type contraption that Joe Cook used in one of his vaudeville acts, c. 1915. 9″ x 7″.

Photograph of a vaudeville theatre featuring Joe Cook, c. 1920. 7 ½″ x 9 ½″.

Trick guitar used by Joe Cook, c. 1920. 41″ x 17″ x 6″.

Ziegfeld

French poster advertising Parisian music hall singer Anna Held, c. 1895. 43 ¾″ x 34 ½″.

Window card featuring Anna Held in *Papa's Wife*, 1899, Strobridge Litho Co., Cincinnati and New York. 23″ x 17″.

Sheet music featuring music from *The Ziegfeld Follies of 1913*, as sung by Elizabeth (Fanny) Brice. 13 ¾″ x 10 ½″.

Sheet music from the Ziegfeld production *Whoopee* starring Eddie Cantor, 1928. 12 ¼″ x 9 ¼″.

*Sheet music featuring a 1914 Ziegfeld Girl. 13 ½″ x 10 ½″. (Illustrated p.20)

Photograph of Adelaide and Albert Gloria, c. 1920. 14″ x 11″.

Photograph of Adelaide Gloria, c. 1915. 14″ x 11″.

Photograph of Adelaide and Albert Gloria in a dance number from a musical revue, c. 1920. 12″ x 9″.

Photographs of the performers of a musical revue, including Adelaide and Albert Gloria (4th and 5th from the left), c. 1920. 12″ x 9″.

Autographed photographs of Ziegfeld Girl Pauline, c. 1915; Alice Lloyd, 1922; and Ziegfeld Girl Vivienne, c. 1920. Each 12″ x 9″.

Movies

Souvenir program for D.W. Griffith's *The Birth of A Nation*, 1915. 12″ x 9 ½″.

Poster for *Your Wife and Mine*, Tripod Pictures Inc., c. 1915. 48″ x 27 ½″.

*Poster for *The Shielding Shadow*, Astra Film Corp., c. 1916. 40″ x 28″. (Illustrated p.22)

Poster for *Fido's Fate*, Triangle Keystone, c. 1915. 39 ½″ x 25″.

Poster for *Burning Sands* at Proctor's Theatre, Troy, N.Y., c. 1920. 36″ x 24″.

Inaugural program from the Strand Theatre, Albany, N.Y., August 13, 1931. 12 ½″ x 9 ½″.

Sheet music for *Goodbye Boys* as featured by Al Jolson, 1913. 13 ¾″ x 10 ½″.

*Illustrated in this catalog